This America
by Lyndon B. Johnson

Photographed by Ken Heyman

A Ridge Press Book

Random House, New York

EDITORIAL DIRECTORS: Robert L. Bernstein, Jerry Mason.
ART DIRECTOR: Albert Squillace. EDITORS: Adolph Suehsdorf, James H. Silberman.
ASSOCIATE EDITORS: Moira Duggan, Frances Foley, Margaret Kane Geer.
ART ASSOCIATES: Allan Mogel, David Namias. ART PRODUCTION: Doris Mullane.

STAFF FOR KEN HEYMAN:
PHOTOGRAPHIC RESEARCH: Natalie Smith. PHOTOGRAPHIC PROCESSING: George Martin.

PUBLISHERS' NOTE On May 22, 1964, a revolution in contemporary American life began. On that day President Lyndon B. Johnson spoke to the graduating class of the University of Michigan at Ann Arbor and first outlined the dimensions of the Great Society.

This book undertakes to show the nature of the challenge implicit in the achievement of such a society. All the words the President had written or spoken to explain his philosophy of the Great Society were studied. From them an outline of the book was prepared which also served as guidance for Ken Heyman, the photographer through whose eyes *This America* was to be seen and interpreted.

Heyman, whose recent book, *Family,* was a notable portrait of human relations, traveled the United States for six months. He returned with more than 13,000 pictures. The best of these were correlated with the President's words. Mr. Johnson studied what had been done, and wrote the introductory and concluding texts.

This America by Lyndon B. Johnson

This America by Lyndon B. Johnson

Neither words nor pictures can

freeze America on a printed page. It was a different country only a moment before these pictures were taken; and a moment later it had changed again. We have only an instant's sight, a brief illumination, of a country which is not so much a place as a process. It is this fact of swift and transforming change which is the experience of modern life—and the source of the American dilemma.

All ages and places have known change. Yet even during those historic times when profound movements were in progress—the end of feudalism, the beginning of nationhood—the average man lived with the expectation that the basic condition of life and the world would be much the same for him from birth until death, and also for his children. Today that comforting security is gone. We are the first generation to know with certainty that life will be different for our children, and even for ourselves, in a few years' time.

Can we accept and welcome the fruits of change while mastering its darker consequences? We become an increasingly urban nation, yet our cities swell to bursting under the pressures of this growth. We want industry and automobiles, yet their products are poisoning the waters of the land and the air we breathe. We demand new machinery to lessen the burdens of labor, yet we must find useful work for increasing numbers.

We welcome the knowledge which takes us on ever farther journeys into space, on ever deeper probes into the process of life itself; yet our educational system creaks under the strain of equipping our young for such a world. On almost every front of human activity the change which enlarges our horizon also menaces our well-being.

There is a second face to our dilemma at once more subtle and more dangerous. Change not only puts up buildings, builds computers, and sends men into space; it also tears down institutions and values and beliefs.

The community—the place where each individual knows his neighbors and has a sense of his own belonging— is being eroded as our cities grow larger and more impersonal. The growing gap between the common experience of the generations threatens the family. The complexity of machines and the enormity of our society leave the individual frustrated in the presence of forces he feels far too weak to master or even influence. Can we preserve old values amid the constant search for the new?

I believe that a great society can master its dilemmas. It begins with the ancient ideal that each citizen must have an equal chance to share the abundance man has created. It is committed to striking racial injustice from the pages of American life and remedying the results of this enormous wrong. It seeks to lift those who have been buried in poverty because of lack of education, or bad health, or blighted environment. It offers the chance to work and live the decent life which a rich and just country owes to all its people.

But the quest for equality does not set the bounds of our task. We will not succeed if every American has his fair share of polluted air or crowded cities or congested schools. It will not be enough to allow everyone an equal chance to be afraid in his streets, or feel frustration at his own insignificance, or be a stranger to other men.

I know that government cannot resolve all these problems. It cannot make men happy or bring them spiritual fulfillment. But it can attempt to remedy the public failures which are at the root of so many of these human ills.

All our domestic programs and policies converge on a common set of aims: to enrich the quality of American life; to provide a living place which liberates rather than constricts the human spirit; to give each of us the opportunity to stretch his talents; and to permit all to share in the enterprise of our society.

A nation is not great simply because it is large or wealthy or powerful. The entire population of ancient Athens could be tucked away in a corner of a large American city, yet its achievements have illumined the life of man for thousands of years. The measure of our own success will be the extent to which we free our people to realize what their imagination and energy can achieve.

The rest is up to them. And if they are a great people, as I believe they are, we will have a great society.

———————————————————————————

The Great Society leads us along
three roads: growth and justice
and liberation. First is growth—the national
prosperity which supports the well-being
of our people and which provides the tools of
our progress. The second road is justice.
Justice means a man's hope should
not be limited by the color of his skin.

The third path is the path of liberation. It is to use our success for the fulfillment of our lives. A great nation is one which breeds a great people. A great people flowers not from wealth and power, but from a society which spurs it to the fullness of its genius. That alone is a great society.

For this is what America is all about. It

e uncrossed desert and the unclimbed ridge.

It is the harvest that i

leeping in the unplowed ground.

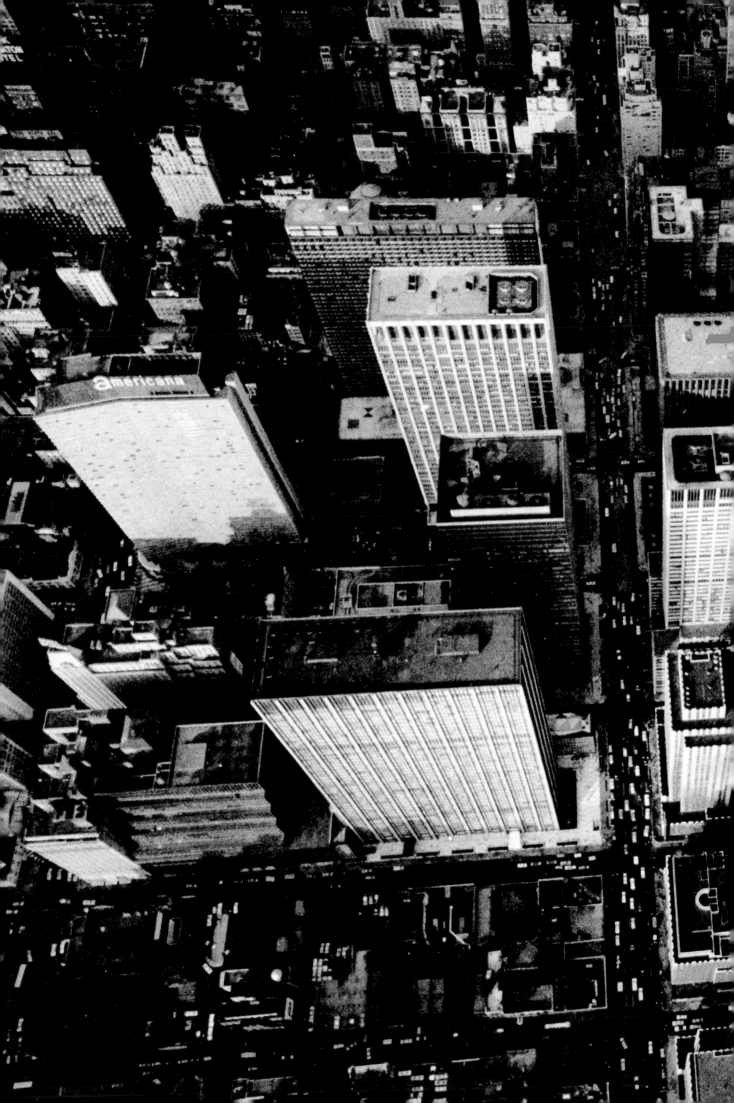

This kind of society
will not flower spontaneously
from swelling riches
and surging power. It will not
be the gift of government or the
creation of Presidents.

For we are a nation of believer

the rush of our day's pursuits, we are believe

Union we believe that every man must son

nderneath the clamor of building and
justice and liberty and union. And in our own
y be free. And we believe in ourselves.

The wonder of nature is the treasure of Americ

The Great Society is a place where leisu

a welcome chance to build and reflect.

The beaut

o

our lan

is

natura

resourc

It

preservatio

is linke

to th

inner prosperit

of th

huma

spiri

Association
with beauty
can
enlarge
man's
imagination
and revive his
spirit.
Ugliness
can demean the
people
who live
in it.

Rural America is the scene of one
of the greatest productive triumphs in the
history of man. Yet, despite its
service to the nation, some parts of rural
America are also the scene of wasted
human talent, where there are too many
people without jobs and too many
with only part-time jobs.

The rural unemployed and
underemployed are largely out of sight.
Most of them are hidden in the remote valleys
of Appalachia and the Ozarks, on the
unpaved side roads of the South,
in the once-rich timber lands of the North,
on Indian reservations, and in the
worn-out mining communities of the West.

If we succeed, it will not be because

nat we have, but because of what we are. 37

In a land of great wealth, famili

In a land rich in harves

ust not live in hopeless poverty.

ildren must not go hungry.

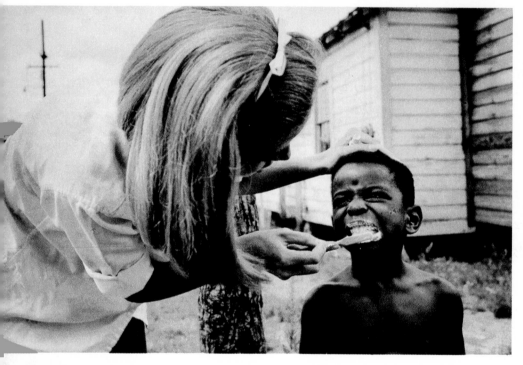

Our job is to open new
vistas—to guide the
young, to comfort the sick,
to teach the skills that
may lead to a more satisfying
and rewarding life.

We will not permi
any part of this country
to be a prison wher
hopes are crushed
The promise of Americ
cannot be denied

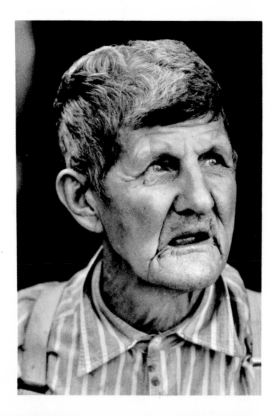

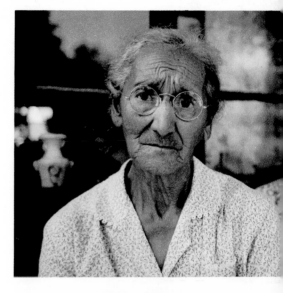

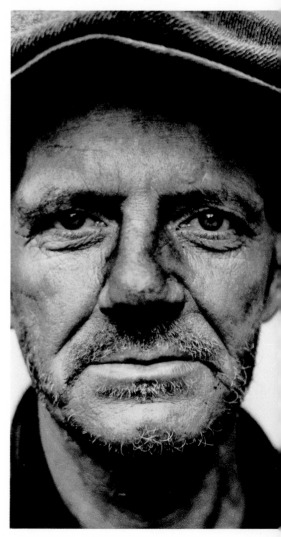

We must provide for every person of advancing a

e dignity and care that honorable years deserve.

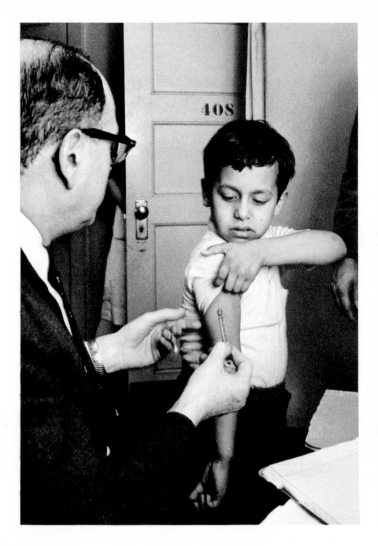

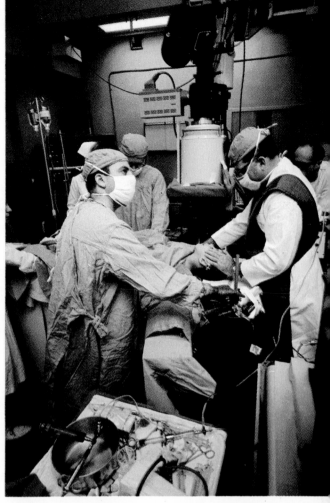

W e cannot close
the dark
corridor of pain
through which sufferers
must pass. But we
can do all that
is humanly possible…

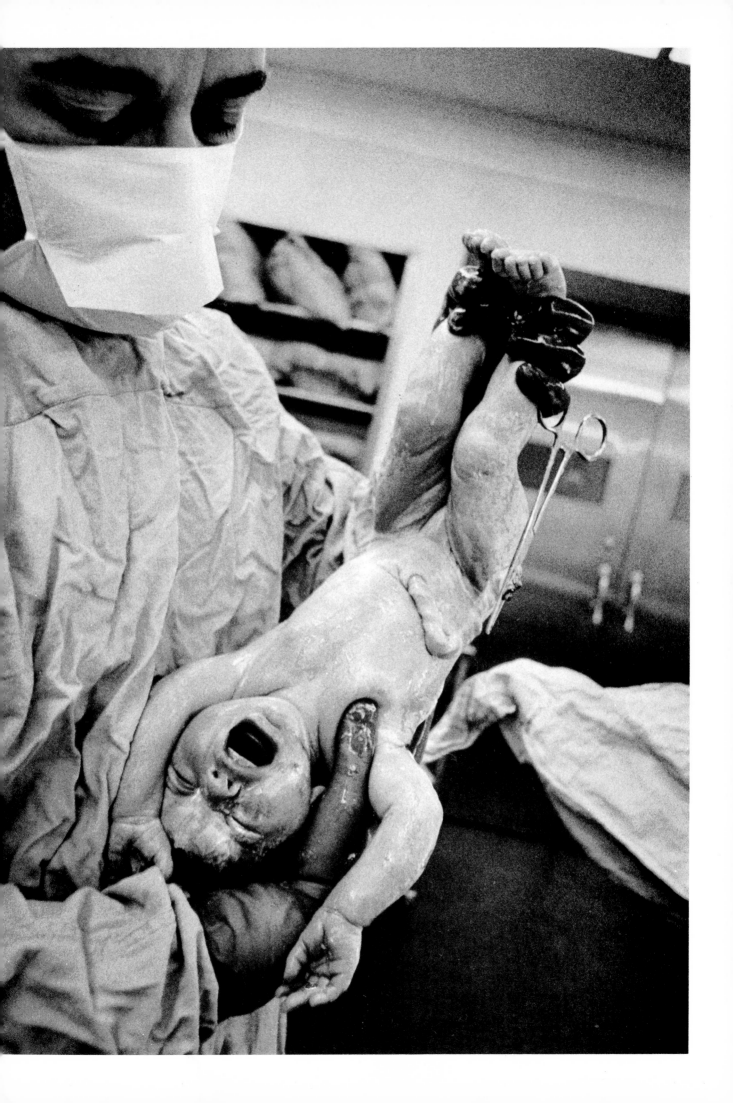

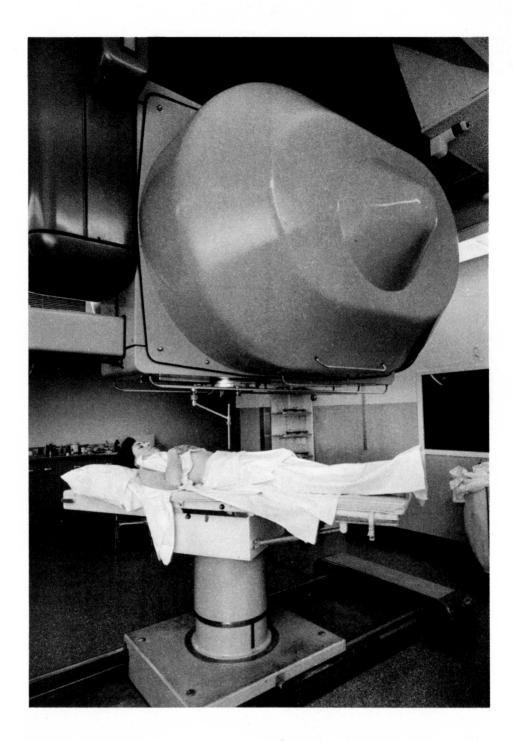

to increase knowledge of these diseases—to less

ffering and reduce the waste of human lives.

In a land of healing miracles, neighbo

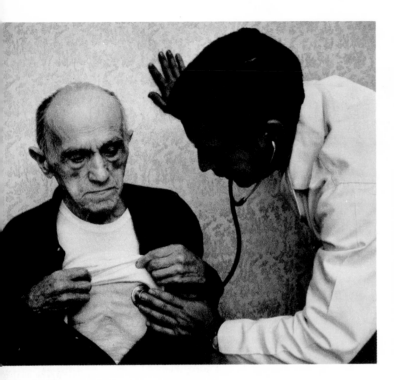

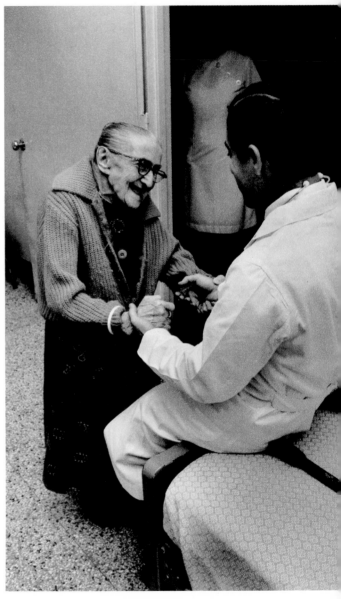

ust not suffer and die untended.

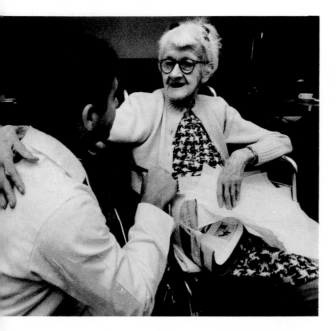

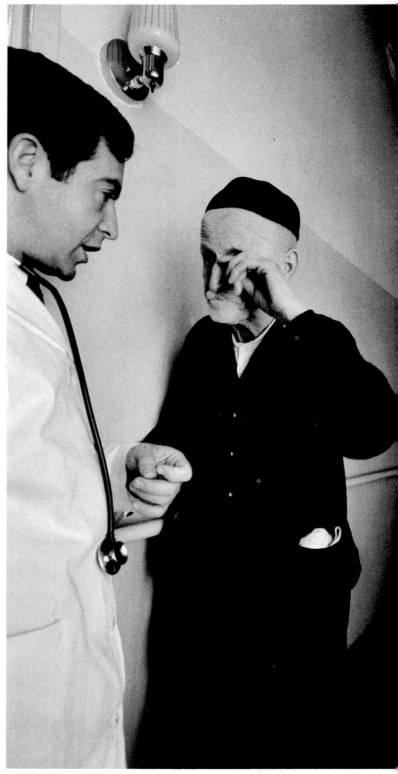

In unity our strength lies and

ity our hope for success rests.

So let us never forget
that unity is the legacy of our
American democracy.
Through the veins of America flows
the blood of all
mankind—from every
continent, every culture,
every creed.

Every child
who learns, and
every man who finds work
and every sick body
made whole
—like a candle
added to an altar—
brightens
the hope of all
the faithful

In a great land of learning
and scholars, young people must be
taught to read and write.

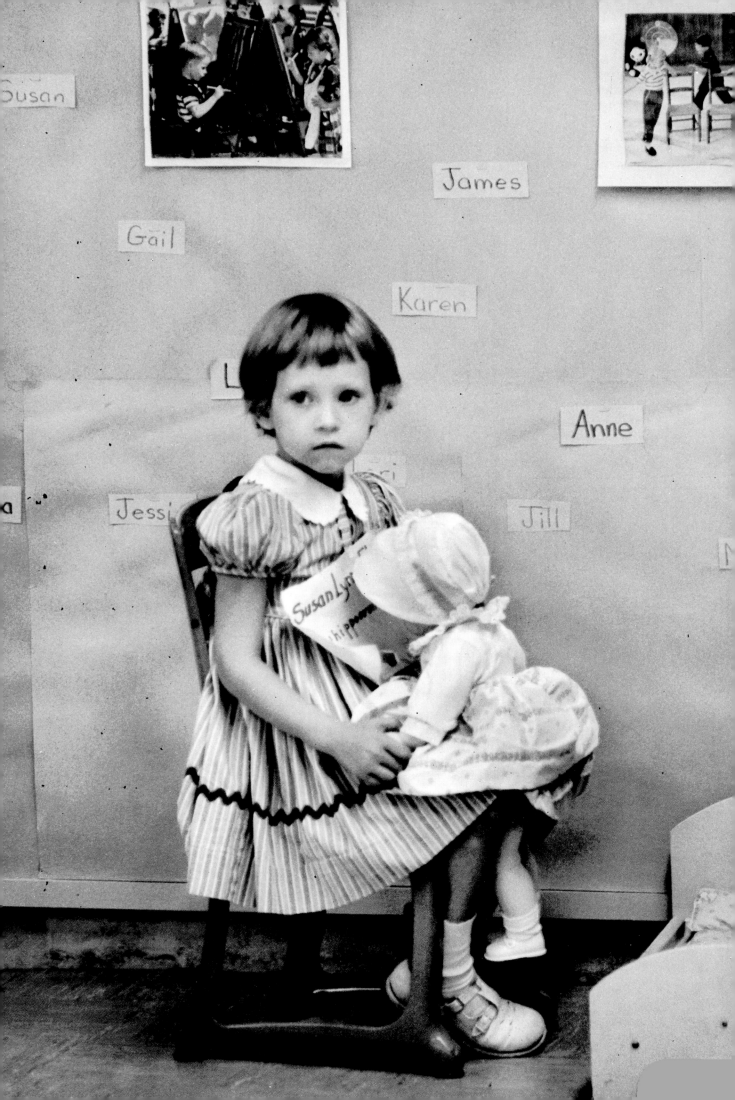

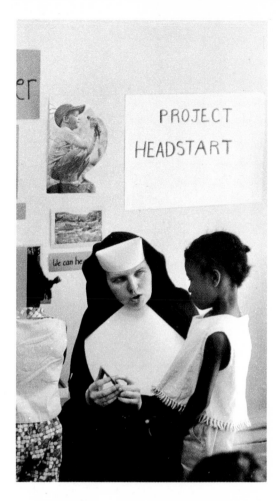

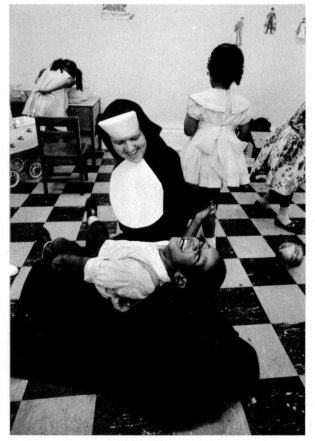

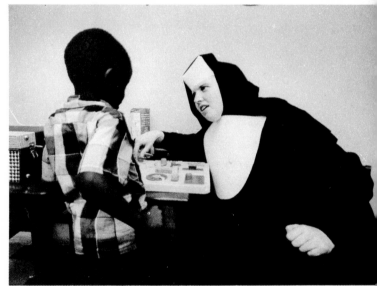

Poverty has
many roots, but
the taproot is
ignorance.

Every child must
have the best
education this nation
can provide.

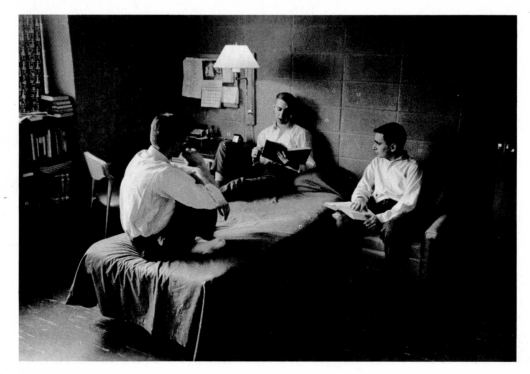

The ultimate defense
of freedom
lies not in
weapons systems or
in the implements
of arms.
These we must maintain.
But freedom's
surest defense, and
freedom's
greatest force,
is the enlightenment
of the minds
of all the people.
Arms can never make us
invulnerable, but
the support that
we give
to education
can make freedom
irresistible.

In the life of the individu

ucation is always an unfinished task.

An educated and healthy people requires surroundings in harmony with its hopes. The city is not an assembly of shops and buildings. It is not a collection of goods and services. Within the borders of our urban centers can be found the most impressive achievements of man's skill and the highest expressions of man's spirit, as well as the worst examples of degradation and cruelty and misery to be found in modern America. The American city should be a collection of communities where every member has a right to belong. It should be a place where every man feels safe on his streets and in the house of his friends. It should be a place where each individual's dignity and self-respect are

strengthened by the respect and
affection of his neighbors. It should be
a place where each of us
can find the satisfaction and warmth
which come only from being
a member of the community of man.
Such a challenge will not be met with a
few more parks or playgrounds.
It requires attention to
the architecture of buildings,
the preservation of historical sites
and monuments, the careful
planning of new suburbs. The first
step is to break old patterns—to begin
to think and work and plan for the
development of the entire metropolitan area.
Our task is to create and preserve
the sense of community with others
which gives us significance and
security, and a sense of
sharing in the common life.

In our time
two giant and
dangerous
forces are
converging on
our cities:
the forces of
growth
and
of decay.

In the next thirty-five years,
we must literally build a
second America—putting in place
as many houses, schools,

apartments, parks, and offices as we
have built through all
the time since the Pilgrims arrived
on these shores.

The quality and condition of our lives are inexorably fixed by the nature of the community in which we live. Slums and ugliness, crime and congestion, growth and decay inevitably touch the lives of all.

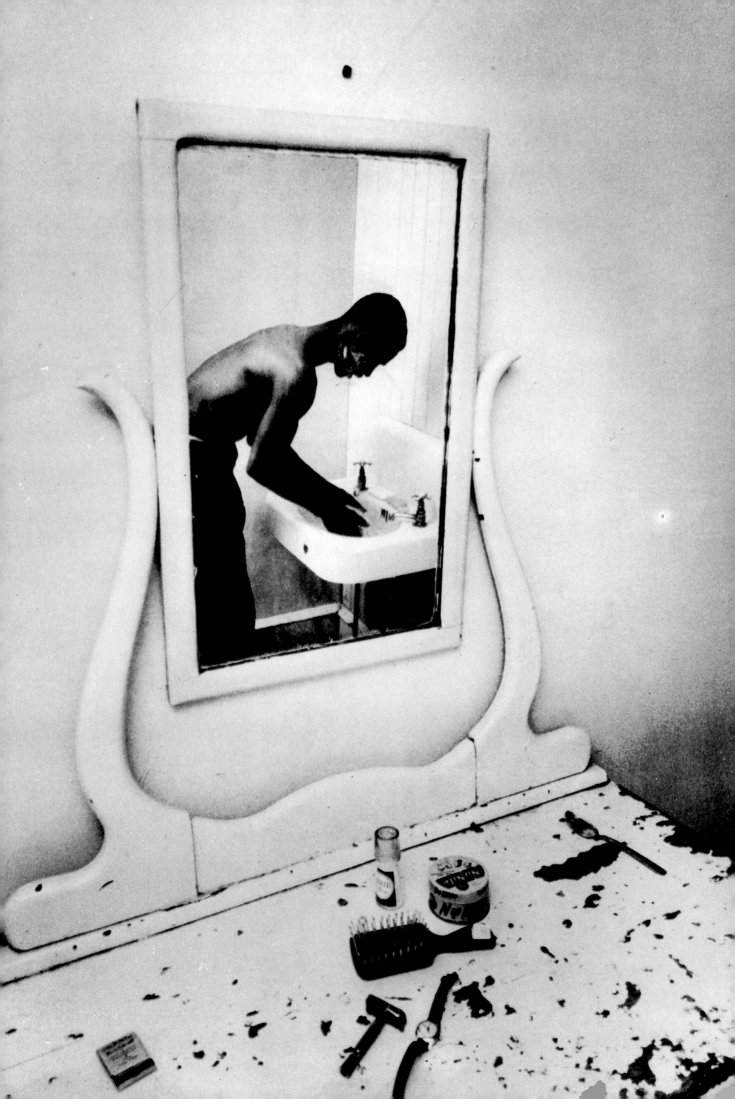

Confined within the discomforts
of noise and ugliness, surrounded by decayed
buildings and despoiled landscapes,

these people of ours yearn for beauty, and hunger for the opportunity to find refreshment in nature.

To make our cities
livable will require the commitment of our
best minds, our selfless
determination, our willingness to
explore new dimensions of
planning and new methods of coordinating
what we know about man and
what we know about
man's
environment.

In short, we can build a new America whe

with nature, drawing strength fro

r people can live in peace and harmony

beauty and wisdom from its variety.

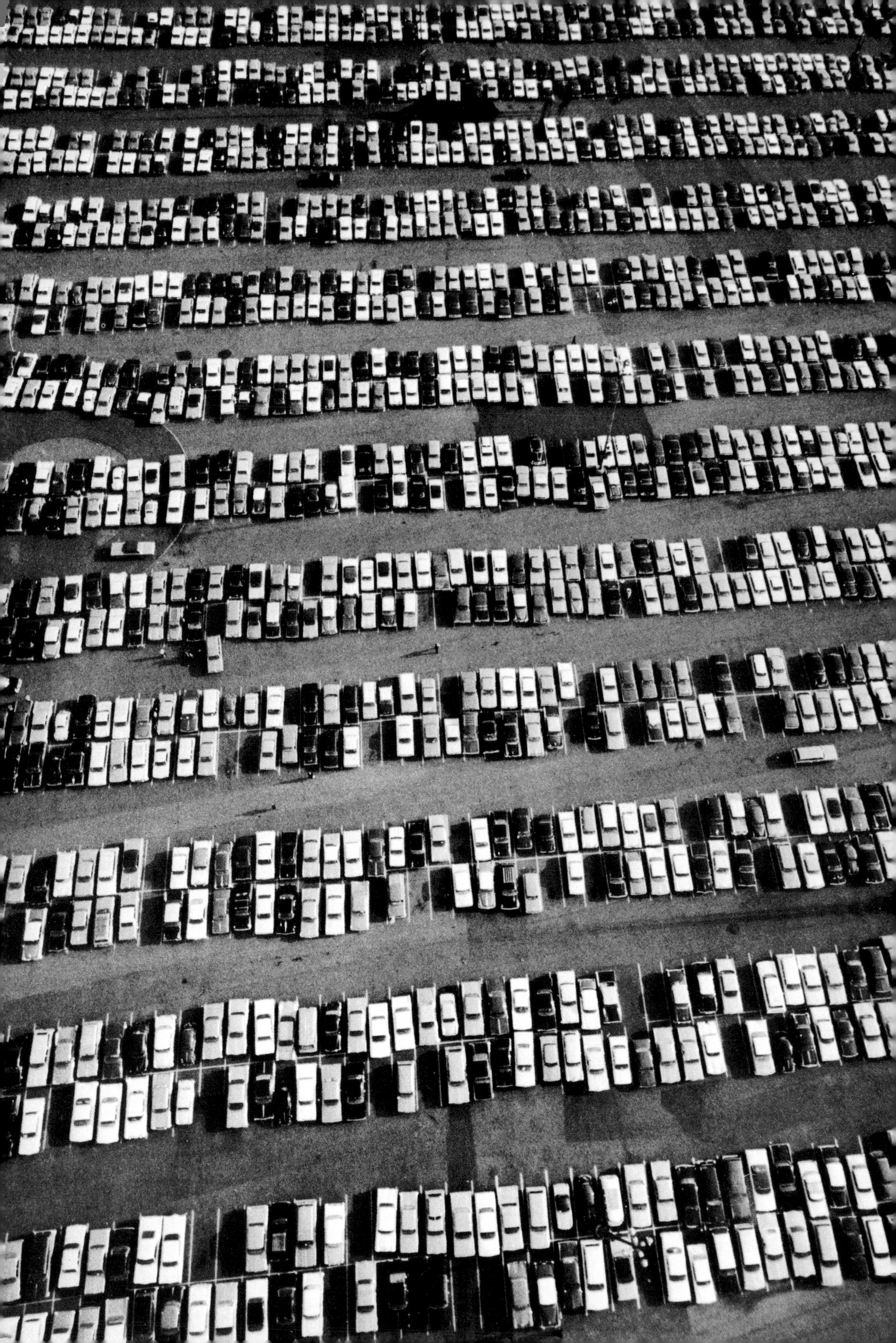

n a day when our astronauts

an circle the globe in less time than

nany Americans spend driving

o and from work, our challenge is real,

nd it is serious,

nd it is urgent.

To split the atom, to launch
the rocket, to explore the innermost
mysteries and the outermost
reaches of the universe—these are
our God-given chores.
And even when you risk bringing
fresh disorder to the
politics of men and nations, these
explorations still must go on.

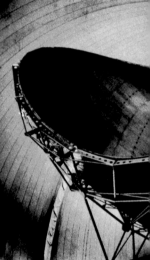

If world conditions were largely
satisfactory it would not be difficult
to evolve a rule of law.
But we do not live in a satisfactory world.
It is stained with evil and

injustice, by ruthless ambition and passionate conflict. Only by fighting these forces can we help to build a base on which the temple of law may rest.

It is America's promise to every
citizen that he shall share in the dignity
of man. This dignity cannot be found
in a man's possessions or in
his power or position. It rests on his
right to be treated as a man
equal in opportunity to all others.
It says he shall share in
freedom, choose his leaders, educate his
children, and provide for his
family according to his ability and
his merits as a human being.
All Americans must have
these privileges of citizenship
regardless of race—not because laws
require it, but because our
conscience commands it. For men
are shaped by their world.

When it is a world of decay, ringed by an invisible wall, when escape is arduous and uncertain, and the saving pressures of a more hopeful society are unknown, it can cripple the youth and desolate the man. Thus, when any citizen denies his fellow, saying: "His color is not mine," or, "His beliefs are strange and different," in that moment he betrays America. And even if we should defeat every enemy and double our wealth and conquer the stars, if we still are unequal to this challenge we will have failed as a people and as a nation. A century has passed since the day of promise. The time of justice now has come.

Every American citizen must
have an equal right to vote. There is no
reason which can excuse the denial
of that right. There is no duty which weighs
more heavily on us than the duty
to ensure that right.

Our fate as
a nation and our future
as a people
rest not upon one
citizen but
upon all citizens.

thout the health, education, and skills…

... that will give him an
opportunity to be an effective citizen and
a self-supporting individual.

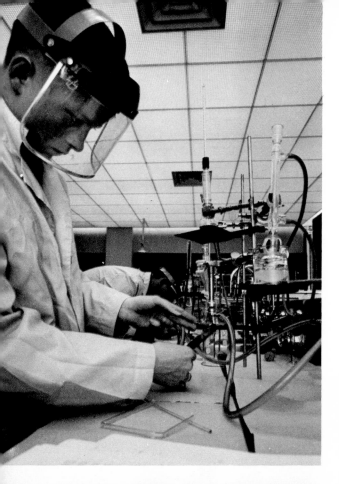

W e will not be
satisfied until every man
knows the dignity
of work and
every man understands the
rewards of labor.

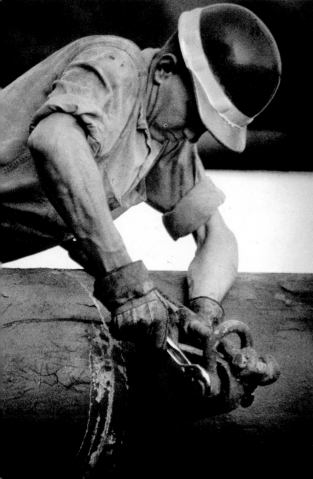

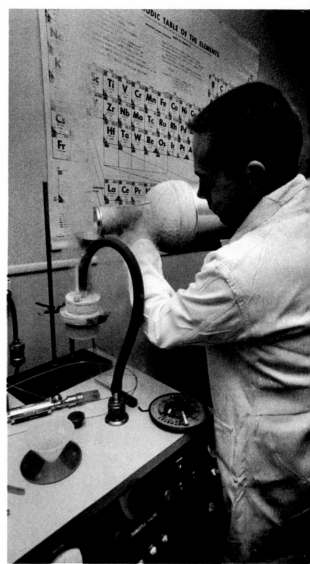

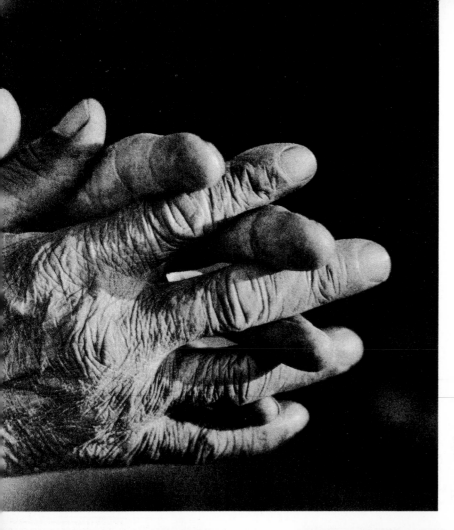

There
ought to be
a job
for
every man
willing
to work.

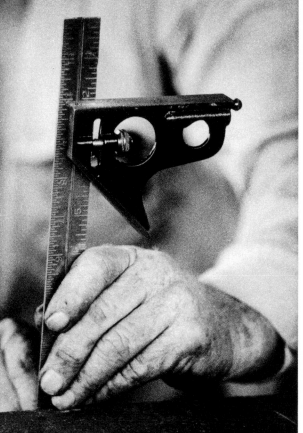

Of all the reckless
devastations of our natural
heritage, none is
more shameful than the
continued poisoning of our
rivers and our air.

Since the beginning of time, fresh water has been one of humanity's most precious needs. For it many wars have been fought. Without it whole civilizations have vanished from the earth.

...this thirsty continent

The farm people of this
nation have made and are continuing
to make a lasting contribution
to our national prosperity.
As a matter of simple
justice they should share
equitably in this prosperity.
They deserve a place
of dignity and opportunity.

The bounty of the
earth is the foundation
of our economy.

We can bring
increased meaning
to our lives if
we are bold enough
to change old
ways—and if the
dream is dear
enough to call forth
the limitless
capacities of
our people.

...a man's footprints on his own soil

We must also
recognize and encourage
those who can be
pathfinders for the nation's
imagination
and understanding.
It is important
that our material prosperity
liberate
and not confine the
creative spirit.

Once a nation commits itself
to the increase and diffusion of knowledge,
the real revolution begins. It
can never be stopped. For despite the
noise of daily events, history is made by
men and the ideas of men.

Our beautiful America
was built by a nation of strangers.
When the earliest settlers poured into a
wild continent there was no one to
ask them where they came from.
The only questions were
Were they sturdy enough to make the journey,
were they strong enough to clear
the land, were they enduring enough to make
a home for freedom, and were they
brave enough to die for liberty if it
became necessary to do so.

What we can do as
world leaders for freedom
depends tomorrow,
as it did yesterday, on
getting our affairs
in order here at home.
This we must do and this
we are going to do.

The work must be our work now.
Scarred by the weaknesses of man,
with whatever guidance God may offer us,
we must strive to ennoble the
life of man on earth.

I have spoken of <u>this</u> America.

I have spoken and written of her problems and her promise. I believe that our destiny as a nation depends upon how well we fulfill the pledges to ourselves: the pledge of freedom, of equality, of a more decent life for all.

What we accomplish around the world will be shaped in large part by what we are and what we become at home. Neither high ideals nor great wealth nor military might will profit us much if we are powerless to solve the problems of our own land.

But we would be shortsighted to confine our vision to this nation's shorelines. The blessings we count at home cannot be cultivated in isolation from the worldwide yearnings of men. An America rich and strong beyond description, yet living in a hostile and despairing world, would be neither safe nor free.

Today the citizens of many nations walk in the shadow of misery. Half the world's adults have never been to school. More than half the world's people are hungry or malnourished. In the developing nations, thousands die daily of cholera, smallpox, malaria and yellow fever —diseases that can be controlled or prevented. Across the world, millions of questioning eyes are turned upon us. What answers can we give?

We mean to show that our dream of a great society does not stop at the water's edge, that it is not just an American dream. All are welcome to share in it and all are invited to contribute to it. The most urgent work of our time— the most urgent work of all time—is to give that dream reality.

The course we follow today traces directly over the two decades since the Second World War. We emerged from that conflict with the sure knowledge that our fate was bound up with the fate of all. Men could no longer content themselves in pursuing narrowly national goals. Men must join in the common pursuit of freedom and fulfillment.

In that pursuit, we have helped Western Europe rebuild, aided Greece and Turkey, come to the defense of Berlin, resisted aggression in Korea and South Vietnam.

In that pursuit, we have helped new nations toward independence, extended the brotherly hand of the Peace Corps, and carried forward the largest program of economic assistance in the history of mankind.

Today, we follow five continuing principles in our policy:

The first principle is to employ our power purposefully, although always with great restraint. In a world where violence remains the prime policy of some, we as surely shape the future when we withdraw as when we stand firm before the aggressor. We can best measure the success of this principle by a simple proposition: not a single country where we have helped mount a major effort to resist aggression today has a government servile to outside interests.

The second principle is to control, to reduce, and ultimately to eliminate the modern engines of destruction. We must not despair or grow cynical at man's efforts to become master of his own fearsome devices. We must push on to harness atomic power as a force for creation rather than destruction.

The third principle is to support those associations of nations which reflect the opportunities and necessities of the modern world. By strengthening the common defense, by stimulating commerce, by confirming old ties and setting new hopes, these associations serve the cause of orderly progress.

A fourth important principle is to encourage the right of each people to govern themselves and shape their own institutions. Today the urge toward independence is perhaps the strongest force in our world. A peaceful world order will be possible only when each country walks the way it has chosen for itself.

A final, enduring strand of our policy as a nation is to help improve the life of man. From the Marshall Plan to now that policy has rested upon the claims of compassion and common sense—and on the certain knowledge that only people with rising faith in the future will build secure and peaceful lands. Not only compassion, but our vital self-interest compels us to play a leading role in a worldwide campaign against hunger, disease, and ignorance.

Half a century ago, William James declared that mankind must seek a "moral equivalent of war." Today the search continues, more urgent than ever before in history. Ours is the great opportunity to challenge all nations, friend and foe alike, to join this battle. We can generate growing light in our universe, or we can allow the darkness to gather. To spread the light, to enlarge man's inner and outer liberty, to promote the peace and well-being of our people and all people—these are the ambitions of my years in office.

They are the enduring purpose, I believe, of this America.